OET Preparation:
English For Healthcare Professionals
Book 1

OET Preparation: English For Healthcare Professionals Book 1

Virginia Allum

Virginia Allum
2018

Copyright © 2018 by Virginia Allum

All rights reserved. This book or any portion thereof may not be reproduced or used in any manner whatsoever without the express written permission of the publisher except for the use of brief quotations in a book review or scholarly journal.

First Printing: 2018

ISBN 978-0-244-06923-0

www.oetprep.com

Virginia Allum

Contents

The Language used in Healthcare 3
Learning New Terms 6
Communication Strategies 15
Hospital Documentation 24
Medical Terms: The Head – Anterior 26
Medical Terms: The Head – posterior 28
Medical Terms: The Face 30
Medical Terms: The Nose 31
Medical Terms: The Eye 33
Medical Terms: The Ear 36
Medical Terms: The Mouth 38
Medical Terms: Anterior of the Chest 40
Medical Terms: Shoulders 42
Medical Terms: The Lower Back 44
Medical Terms: The Buttocks 46
Medical Terms: Thigh and Hips..48
Medical Terms: Abdominopelvic Region...50
Medical Terms: Anterior Knee and Lower Leg 52
Medical Terms: Posterior Lower Leg and Knee 54
Medical Terms: The Foot 57
Medical Terms: The Arms 59
Medical Terms: Back of the Hand 61
Medical Terms: Palm of the Hand 62
Medical Terms: Fingernails and Toenails 65
Answers: 67

OET Preparation: English for Healthcare Professionals Book 1

Virginia Allum

The Language used in Healthcare

Everyday versus Medical Terms

Doctors and nurses use several different levels of language when communicating with patients and when talking with other colleagues. There are two main levels of language that are used. These are:

Everyday expressions

Every day expressions are used for parts of the body or for diseases or conditions when speaking to a lay person. Everyday expressions tend to come from Old English words and are often simple words. Many of the everyday names for parts of the body come from Old English. For example, arm, elbow, shoulder, hand, foot. There are everyday terms for some commonly occurring diseases as well, e.g. heartburn, toothache and foot drop.

Medical terms

Medical terms are often derived from Ancient Greek or Latin as the Ancient Greeks and Romans took a great interest in the human body. Medical terms that are derived from Greek often describe diseases or conditions while words derived from Latin often describe the functions of a body part and may also be used as an adjective form. Medical terminology is more common in written texts but may also be used when healthcare workers speak with colleagues.

Because of the background of the words that are used to describe the body and related diseases or conditions, each body part may have three word roots or base words to describe it. For example, the three base words that are used to describe the *mouth* are:

Old English *'muth'*	Latin *'oro'*	Greek *'stoma'*
mouth	oral	stomatitis
mouthpiece	oropharynx	stomatology
mouth breathing	oropharyngeal	
mouth ulcer		

Virginia Allum

Activity 1: Complete the sentences with words from the table above.

1. Trauma to the mucous membrane of the oral cavity can cause _____.

2. The _____ is also called the back of the throat.

3. The medical term for a sore mouth is _____.

4. The part of a device which is placed in the mouth is called the _____.

5. _____ can cause a dry mouth.

OET Preparation: English for Healthcare Professionals Book 1

Virginia Allum

Learning New Terms

Learning and remembering medical terms is a little like learning a new language. Read the following text about the skills you will use to develop an increasing vocabulary of medical terms.

1. How to learn new terms

There is a certain amount of memorising which is necessary in a Medical English course. Memorising refers to the process of getting information, storing it in the memory and retrieving it later when needed. There are three stages in memorising and retaining information.

Stage 1. The sensory memory

Sensory information is taken in from the environment using your senses - sight, touch, hearing and smell. They are stored for a very short time, usually only a few seconds. Not all of the information is worked on in the brain i.e. thought about. Imagine yourself walking down a street. All the information that you sense goes into your sensory memory. For example, you see some flowers in the garden of number 16 which you'd like to plant in

OET Preparation: English for Healthcare Professionals Book 1

your   own

garden. This information is important to you and you are consciously thinking about it so it will then move to your.....

Stage 2. Short-term or active memory

Most of the information stored in the short-term memory will be stored for around 20 to 30 seconds. Many short-term memories are quickly forgotten. Memories which are worked on actively are not forgotten and continue to your...

Stage 3. Long-term memory

This is your 'memory bank' or the place where information is stored. Memories are arranged in groups or clusters so they are ready for you to recall.

Tips you can use to improve your ability to retain information and memorise important information:

1.Work with reasonable chunks of information. Do not expect to memorise pages of terms in one go. It is better to work with 3-5 new terms each day and end up with 21 -35 new terms a week than try to learn 35 new terms in a day.

Remember to contextualise the term as well by placing the term in a sentence or identifying the term in a text. Medical terms in isolation are not useful and will be difficult to retain.

2. Develop mental images of the terms you want to remember e.g. labelling pictures or photos of equipment associates terms with a sensory memory - a visual memory.

3. Make connections to information you already know. For instance, you may already know that 'appendicectomy' means 'cutting out the appendix' from personal experience. Therefore, you will easily be able to remember that the suffix 'ectomy' means 'to cut out surgically'.

4. Group information. You can use a mind map to create a visual grouping. For example, in learning the names of the main bones of the body, the central term is 'The Body'. The next group of terms which shoot out from the central term are 'head', 'body', 'arm'

OET Preparation: English for Healthcare Professionals Book 1

and 'leg'. Finally, these terms are divided into relevant terms e.g. 'leg' is divided into 'tibia', 'fibula', 'femur' etc.

5. Repetition of information helps to keep information in the short-term memory long enough to be worked on for storage in the long-term memory. Terms should not be repeated in isolation; context is essential or the repetition is meaningless. Activities which are useful are matching activities which match the term with the correct meaning and gap-fill activities.

6. Review terms aloud. Work with online dictionaries to check pronunciation and then repeat the terms aloud. A useful site for help with the pronunciation of medical terms is www.thefreedictionary.com where you can hear both British English pronunciation and American English pronunciations.

Virginia Allum

Types of Nurses

Staff work in specialised areas around the hospital, in long-term care settings such as nursing homes or hostels and also in the community. Nurses work as part of the MDT or Multi-Disciplinary Team which may also include doctors, physiotherapists, social workers, occupational therapists and others depending on need. The levels of nurses may have different names in different countries, for example:

UK	Australia	USA
Ward Manager Charge Nurse	Nursing Unit Manager (NUM)	Nurse Manager
Nurse Sister (Senior)	Registered Nurse RN	Registered Nurse RN
Enrolled Nurse EN	Enrolled Nurse EN	Licensed Vocational Nurse LVN Licensed Practical Nurse LPN
Healthcare Assistant HCA	Assistant in Nursing AIN	Certified Nursing Assistant CNA

OET Preparation: English for Healthcare Professionals Book 1

Names of Nurses

The names of nurses vary from one English-speaking country to another. Their level of qualifications may also vary. This is difficult for easy movement of nurses between countries.

The four main levels of nurses are:

Nursing Assistants may be called Healthcare Assistants (HCAs), Certified Nursing Assistants (CNAs) or Assistants in Nursing. In the UK, nursing assistants who work in nursing homes are called *carers*, in Australia, *Personal Carers (PCs)*. Trained Nursing Assistants will have studied a certificate course in health at a Vocational College.

Enrolled Nurses (ENs) are called **Licensed Practical Nurses (LPNs)** in the USA may work in hospitals or in the community.

Registered Nurses may be called RNs or Nurses. In most countries RNs are required to undertake an undergraduate Nursing degree but some RNs still study a Diploma in Nursing. Some countries are in the process of changing over completely to Bachelor of Nursing requirement for RNs. RNs work in hospital wards or clinics. They work in GP Practices as Practice Nurses and as District Nurses in the Community. In hospitals there are usually several levels of nurses. The names of nurses who are in charge of wards or units may also vary, e.g. in the UK they are called Ward Managers or Charge Nurses if they are male. In Australia, ward managers are called Nursing Unit Managers, abbreviated to NUMs.

Clinical Nurse Specialists (CNS) may work as a specialist in a particular area, e.g. tissue viability.

Nurse Practitioners (NPs) also called **Advanced Nurse Practitioner (ANPs)** may be responsible for the running of a clinic or specialist area. NPs are Registered nurses who make autonomous decisions for which they are accountable.

OET Preparation: English for Healthcare Professionals Book 1

Newer Nursing careers include the following:

- Transitional Care Nurse also called a Discharge Planner
- Forensic Nurse: a nurse with expertise used in criminal cases and medical court cases
- Occupational Health Nurse (OHN): a workplace-based nurse looking after the health of a company's employees
- Travel Health Nurse: a nurse who retrieves sick or injured patients nationally or internationally
- Telehealth Nurse: a nurse who monitors a patient's data remotely, e.g. blood pressure or cardiac monitoring
- Nursing Informatics Nurse: a nurse who uses computer programmes to analyse the needs of patients and staff
- Nursing Researcher: a nurse who is involved in the development of evidence-based research

Virginia Allum

Virginia Allum

Communication Strategies

There are several types of strategies which you can use to improve communication effectiveness with your patients and colleagues. Spoken fluency relates to your ability to produce stretches of language in a natural way. Fluency may be more difficult, if you have to produce language spontaneously without the chance to practise a possible dialogue beforehand, e.g. during emergencies. Effective communication can be helped by learning and practising communication strategies such as:

- using discourse markers
- using fillers
- non-verbal communication
- knowing when to use one way and two way communication
- practising rehearsal techniques
- clarification strategies
- paraphrasing and summarising
- using open-ended questions
- giving instructions in three steps

Discourse markers

words or phrases used in speaking and writing to signal that the speaker or writer wants to communicate an idea. Examples of discourse markers are expressions like 'on the other hand', 'in addition' and 'consequently'. Discourse markers are often quite formal and are therefore used more often in writing.

Fillers

words or phrases that signal that the speaker needs time to think before continuing. Words or phrases like 'You know?', 'Umm', 'Right' cover silences which might otherwise be uncomfortable.

Non-verbal communication

communication which does not rely on words. Examples of non-verbal communication are postures, facial expression, eye gaze, gestures, and tone of voice. Non-verbal communication tends to have a cultural component and may have different meanings in other cultures. Gestures in particular, often have different meanings in different cultures.

One-way communication

information that passes in one direction only, e.g. from a speaker to a listener during an intercom message, in a radio programme or during a lecture. There is often no opportunity to include non-verbal communication in one-way communication.

Two-way communication

verbal and non-verbal information passing back and forth from speaker to listener e.g. regular conversation, discussion between nurse and patient, telephone conversation (some non-verbal communication is possible)

Rehearsal techniques: Preparing yourself for any possible dialogues you may come across is a good way to reduce stress about your ability to manage complex conversations. This means that you research the background to the conversation e.g. pre-assessment of a patient. Predict the vocabulary you will need and practise it.

Clarification strategies: Before clarifying any unknown vocabulary or meaning it is important to look at the overall meaning of the text. The context of the conversation will give clues about the meaning of individual words. If the meaning of the word cannot be guessed this way it is important to clarify the meaning with the speaker. This may be especially important in the healthcare environment e.g. talking about procedures or medication.

Paraphrasing: A summary of what has just been heard by the listener. This is a way for the listener to prove to the speaker that s/he has understood correctly.

Three- step instructions Instructions which include several parts are common, e.g. 'The wound swabs are on the middle shelf of the trolley at the back of the Treatment Room'. Information has to be retained until the end of the instruction. Strategies to be successful in retaining information include numbering the steps in your head and writing notes of the steps.

Virginia Allum

Nursing Procedures

Nursing procedures include taking patient observations, doing an ECG, taking blood sugar levels and doing wound dressings. Each unit includes review of relevant vocabulary and a review of the kinds of language functions which need to be used.

The language functions that you will use are:

- giving instructions
- asking for co-operation
- advising
- recommending
- giving directions

OET Preparation: English for Healthcare Professionals Book 1

Describing nursing activities using make, do and take

Activity 2: Complete the following expressions using *make, do* or *take*. Each verb may be used more than once.

1. _____ a bed
2. _____ an ECG
3. _____ a pulse
4. _____ a blood pressure
5. _____ a blood sugar level
6. _____ a temperature
7. _____ a dressing
8. _____ some blood
9. _____ a urinalysis
10. _____ a referral to the District Nurse

Tests and medical procedures

Medical tests are used in the diagnosis of diseases and conditions. They include:

- **diagnostic tests** which diagnose the presence of diseases or disorders
- **screening tests** which detect the presence of disease in a group of people
- **analysis** of body fluids, e.g. full blood count and urinalysis
- **Medical Imaging** such as X-ray, MRI and CT Scan
- **endoscopy** used to view inner parts of the body using a special microscope
- **laparoscopy and arthroscopy** using Minimally Invasive Surgery
- **biopsy** to examine tissue samples under a microscope

OET Preparation: English for Healthcare Professionals Book 1

Types of Medical Treatment

Activity 3: Match the terms with their correct meanings.

1. disorder	a) abnormal physical or mental condition
2. disease	b) use of a remedy against a disease
3. treatment	c) abnormal function of part of the body
4. diagnosis	d) activity which treats a disease or injury
5. procedure	e) identification of the cause of a disease

Predicting Non-Verbal Communication

Activity 4: Put the terms under the correct headings.

statements   questions   changing body position

gestures   commands   eye contact   interjections

tone of voice

Verbal Communication	Non-Verbal Communication

Virginia Allum

Text Comprehension: Listening Skills

Active and Passive Listening Skills

Developing active and passive listening skills will increase the amount of information which you can understand. Active Listening skills help you predict the content of a communication. Developing the readiness to listen means it is easier to hear the key points of a conversation. It also increases sensitivity to non-verbal communication. Also, listening for key words which the speaker stresses naturally helps give clues about the content of the communication.

Passive Listening includes listening to everyday texts such as radio programmes and also authentic texts such as lectures or online videos. Listening to a variety of accents and dialects helps to acclimatise the listener to the sounds of English.

Many radio and TV websites have video clips which include transcripts of the programmes. By downloading and printing the transcript students can listen to the video and follow the transcript at the same time.

OET Preparation: English for Healthcare Professionals Book 1

Hospital Documentation

Texts may be both written and verbal. There are many different types of written texts which are used in hospitals. Many of the documents are pre-printed documents that are completed by ticking a box or initialling to confirm an activity has been completed. This is the case with care pathways and care plans. Care pathways are also called Integrated Care Pathways, Clinical Pathways or simply pathways.

Care Pathways are set out as a list of nursing duties for each day of care. Nurses initial each activity each shift as they perform the nursing duties. Any section which cannot be completed is called a 'Variance'. The reasons for variances in care are explained on the Communication Page of the pathway.

Documentation such as policies and procedures forms, reports or hospital memos are written as information texts which do not require any written input from the reader. At most, nurses may have to sign after reading the text to confirm that they have read and understood the text.

Charts such as temperature charts or diabetes charts usually require the recording of number values with little other writing. Abbreviations are commonly found on these sorts of charts, e.g. 'BP' meaning blood pressure and 'bsl' meaning blood sugar level.

Finally, the patient record or nursing notes is the main area of writing which nurses will complete in prose. Abbreviations are acceptable in the patient record, as long as they are clear and have been approved by the hospital. Some nurses enter patient notes on computerised patient records, but this is by no means standard.

Medical Terms: The Body

Medical Terms: The Head – Anterior

Term	Latin	Greek
head	caput	cephalo
hair	pilus	tricho
skull	cranium	
forehead	fronto	
temple	temporalis	
jaw		gnatho
upper jaw	maxilla	
lower jaw	mandibula	
neck	cervix	

Activity 1: Label the picture.
head   crown   hair   forehead   temple   chin

Virginia Allum

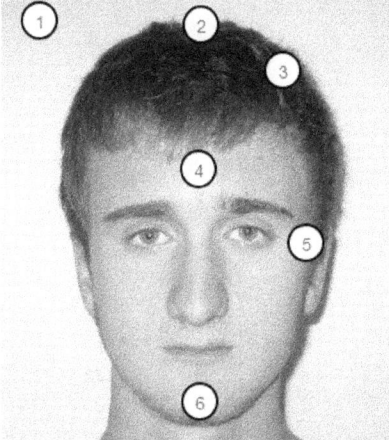

1.
2.
3.
4.
5.
6.

Activity 2: Complete the information about diseases and conditions of the anterior head. Note: -dynia = pain

gnathodynia   maxillofacial   craniotomy

    cephalic   trichotillomania

1. A _____ presentation in childbirth is also called 'head first'.

2. Compulsive hair pulling is known as _____.

3. During a _____, a bone flap is removed from the skull to gain access to the brain.

4. Pain in the jaw is called _____.

OET Preparation: English for Healthcare Professionals Book 1

Medical Terms: The Head – posterior

Term	Latin	Greek
crown	corona capitis	
back of the head	occiput	
side of the head	parietal	
nape of the neck	nucha	

Activity 3: Label the picture.
crown   occiput   parietal side   nape   ear lobe

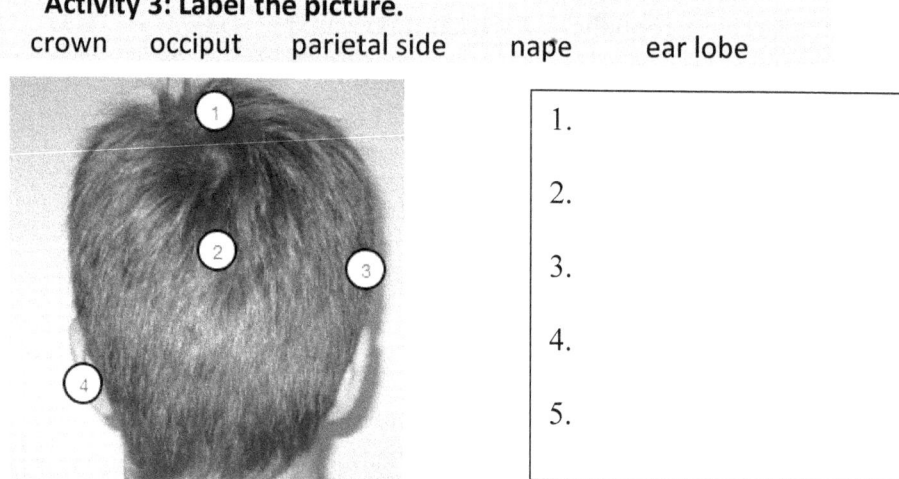

1.
2.
3.
4.
5.

Virginia Allum

Activity 4: Complete the information about diseases and conditions of the posterior of the head.

| crown | back | nuchal |

1. Hair thinning or alopecia is sometimes seen on the _____ of the head.

2. Occipital neuralgia is a type of pain felt in the _____ of the head.

3. A _____ scan is a type of antenatal scan of the nape of the neck, used to identify chromosomal abnormalities in babies.

OET Preparation: English for Healthcare Professionals Book 1

Medical Terms: The Face

Term	Latin	Greek
face	facio	
cheeks (inside)	bucca	
cheekbone		zygoma
mouth	os/oris	stoma
Adam's apple		laryngeal prominence

Virginia Allum

Activity 5: Label the picture.
Adam's apple   nose   face   cheekbone   mouth

1.
2.
3.
4.
5.

Activity 6: Complete the information about diseases and disorders of the face.

1. The _____ cavity, includes the buccal cavity (area between teeth, cheek and gums).

2. A blow to the cheek may result in a fractured_____ or cheekbone,

3. Genioplasty is a type of cosmetic surgery, where _____ implants are inserted into the chin to reshape the line of the lower face

Medical Terms: The Nose

Term	Latin	Greek
nose	naso	rhino
nostril	naris	
nostrils	nares	
bridge of the nose	nasal dorsum	
side of the nose	ala nasi	
sides of the nose	alae nasi	
nasal septum	columella	
nasal hair	vibrissa	
nasal hairs	vibrissae	

Virginia Allum

Activity 7: Label the picture.

nostril   glabella   bridge of the nose   ala nasi   nasal septum

1.
2.
3.
4.
5.

Activity 8: Complete the information.

nostril   epistaxis   rhinoplasty   nosebleeds

1. A 'nose job' or _____ means surgical correction of a nasal defect.

2. Nasal sprays instil a fine mist into each _____ to relieve congestion, so patients can breathe more easily.

3. Patients with nasoseptal defects often have difficulty breathing because of recurrent _____.

4. A nosebleed is also called an _____.

Medical Terms: The Eye

Term	Latin	Greek
eye socket	orbit	
eye	occulo	ophthalmos
white of the eye	sclera	
iris		iris
pupil	pupil	
eyeball	bulbus oculi	
eyelid	palpebra	blepharo
corner of the eye	canthus	
vertical crease of skin over canthus	epicanthus	
crease on the upper eyelid	supratarsal fold	
eyelash	cilium	blepharo
eyelashes	cilia	blepharon
eyebrow	supercilium	
space between eyebrows	glabella	

Virginia Allum

Activity 9: Label the picture of the opened eye.

pupil   supratarsal fold   iris   sclera

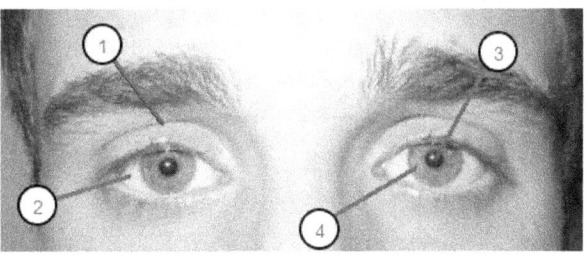

1.
2.
3.
4.

Activity 10: Label the picture of the closed eye.

eye lash   eye brow   canthus   eyelid

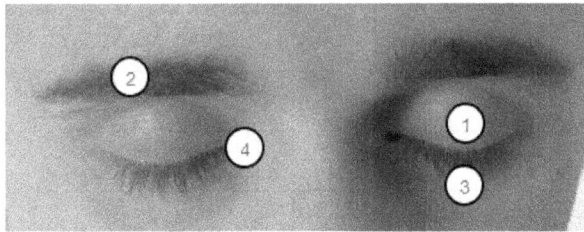

1.
2.
3.
4.

Activity 11: Complete the information.

eye   protect   epicanthus   orbit   eyelid

1. The eye socket or _____ is the cavity where the eyeball sits.

2. The iris is the coloured part of the _____ .

3. The _____ in the centre of the eye, is always black.

4. Blepharoplasty, also called an _____ lift, is performed to remove 'bags under the eyes.'

5. The function of eyelashes is to _____ the eyes from dust or foreign bodies.

6. A vertical skin fold on the inside of the eye, called an _____, is a sign of Down Syndrome.

Medical Terms: The Ear

Term	Latin	Greek
ear	auris	oto
earlobe	lobule of auris	
outer ear	pinna / auricle	
ear wax	cerumen	
ear hairs	cilia	
ear drum	tympanic membrane	

Virginia Allum

Activity 12: Label the picture.

ear lobe   cilia   cerumen   pinna

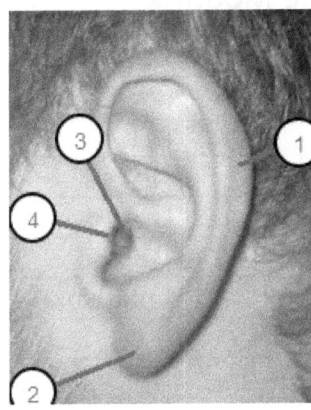

1.
2.
3.
4.

Activity 13: Complete the information.

earache   membrane   build-up   sticky
tubes   insertion   middle ear

Otitis media is an infection of the _____. It is commonly known as glue ear, because of the presence of _____ fluid between the tympanic _____ and the inner ear. Fluid in the Eustachian _____ in the inner ear causes reduced hearing and _____. Treatment includes antibiotics to treat the ear infection and sometimes the _____ of grommets in the ear to allow any _____ of fluid to flow to the outside.

OET Preparation: English for Healthcare Professionals Book 1

Medical Terms: The Mouth

Term	Latin	Greek
roof of the mouth / hard palate	palatum	
uvula / soft palate	uvula	
lips	labia	
tongue	lingua	glosso
throat		pharynx
throat above the collar bone	jugulum	
tooth	dento	
teeth	denti	
tonsils	tonsillae	
gums	gingiva	

Activity 14: Label the picture of the mouth.

uvula   tongue   tooth   gingiva   palate

1.
2.
3.
4.
5.

Virginia Allum

Activity 15: Complete the sentences.

1. Gingivitis is a dental condition, where the _____ are inflamed and show signs of infection.

2. Glossitis or inflammation of the _____ may be a sign of anaemia or poor nutrition.

3. Dentification is the formation of _____ in the gums.

4. Tonsils are lumps of lymphoid _____ found at the back of the mouth.

5. Laser-assisted uvuloplasty (LAUP) is a procedure that repairs the _____ to treat primary snoring.

OET Preparation: English for Healthcare Professionals Book 1

Medical Terms: Anterior of the Chest

Term	Latin	Greek
breast bone	sternum	
breast	masto	mammo
nipple	papilla mammae	
areola	areola mammae	
Montgomery tubercles	areolar tubercles	
chest / chest wall	pectus / stetho	thorax
rib	costo	
space between ribs	intercostal space	
armpit / underarm	axilla	
armpits / underarms	axillae	

Activity 16: Label the picture.
clavicle   sternum   axilla   ribs

1.
2.
3.
4.

Virginia Allum

Activity 17: Label the picture.

nipple   Montgomery tubercles   areola

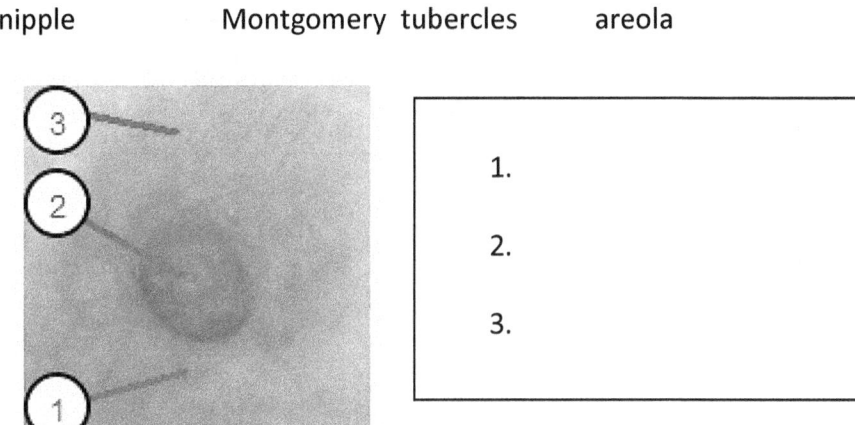

1.

2.

3.

Activity 18: Match the diseases and disorders of the breast.

1. mastopexy	a) surgical removal of a breast
2. mastectomy	b) breast augmentation
3. gynaecomastia	c) cosmetic surgery to lift sagging breasts
4. mammoplasty	d) abnormal breast tissue in men

OET Preparation: English for Healthcare Professionals Book 1

Medical Terms: Shoulders

Term	Latin	Greek
shoulder	humerus	omos
shoulder blade	scapula	
shoulder tip		acromion
neck bones	cervical vertebrae	

Activity 19: Label the picture.

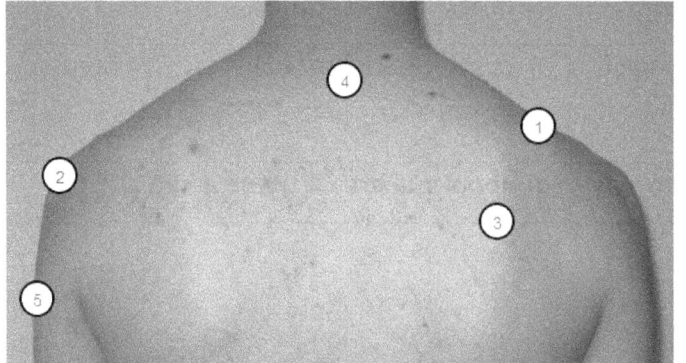

1.
2.
3.
4.
5.

Virginia Allum

Activity 20: Complete the sentences.

deltoid　　　shoulder blades　　　shoulder　　　subacromial

1. ASD or Arthroscopic Subacromial Depression is a procedure which increases the size of the _____ area to reduce pressure on the shoulder muscles.

2. Rotator cuff repair is surgery to repair a torn tendon in the shoulder. The repair is often achieved during _____ arthroscopy.

3. Overuse of the shoulder and arm can cause muscular pain between the _____.

4. The _____ muscle in the upper arm is a site where intramuscular injections may be given.

OET Preparation: English for Healthcare Professionals Book 1

Medical Terms: The Lower Back

Term	Latin	Greek
spine / backbone	vertebrae	rachis / spondylo
lower back	lumbo	
base of the spine	sacrum	
dimples of Venus	fossae lumbales laterales	
tailbone	coccyx	
flank	ilium /latero	

Activity 21: Label the picture.
sacrum   dimple of Venus   flank   lumbar back   spine

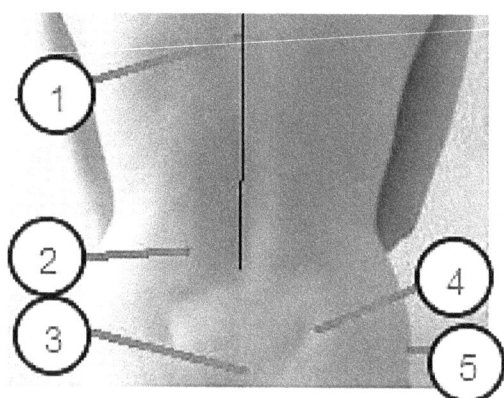

1.

2.

3.

4.

5.

Activity 22: Complete the sentences.

flank   pain   childbirth   landmarks   spine

1. the sacrum is a large, triangular bone at the base of the _____, where pressures can form, if patients are immobile ion bed.

2. Dislocation of the coccyx during _____ can lead to pain and discomfort when sitting.

3. The 'Dimples of Venus' are anatomical _____ which indicate where the sacrum attaches to the pelvis.

4. Body sculpting procedures include liposuction of fat in the lateral _____ area, to reduce 'love handles' or excess fat.

5. Kidney infection can cause flank _____, fever, chills and haematuria.

Medical Terms: The Buttocks

Term	Latin	Greek
buttocks	gluteus	
buttocks crack	gluteal cleft	
gluteal fold	sulcus gluteus	
cheek (of the buttock)	natis	
cheeks	nates	

Activity 23: Label the picture.

gluteal fold   gluteal cleft   sacrum   cheek

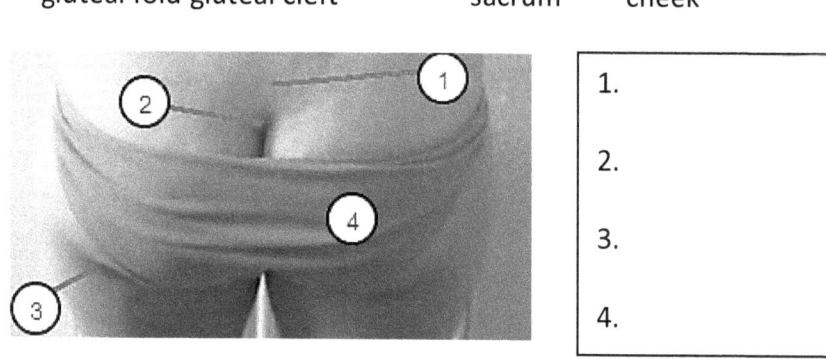

1.
2.
3.
4.

Virginia Allum

Activity 24: Complete the sentences.

1. Uneven gluteal _____ in the buttocks of infants can indicate the condition called hip dysplasia.

2. Pilonidal cysts are abscesses which often form around an ingrown hair in or near the _____.

3. Tightening of the skin of sagging _____ is a cosmetic procedure known as a buttock lift.

OET Preparation: English for Healthcare Professionals Book 1

Medical Terms: Thigh and Hips

Term	Latin	Greek
hip	coxa	ischion
hip bone	os coxae	
thigh	femur	
stretch marks	striae	
groin	inguino	

Virginia Allum

Activity 25: Label the picture.

striae   buttock   waist   external thigh   abdomen   hip

1.
2.
3.
4.
5.
6.

Activity 26: Label the picture.

inner thigh   hip   groin   outer thigh

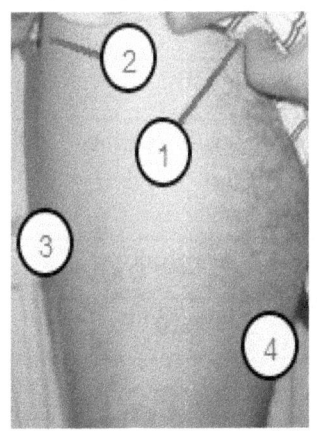

1.
2.
3.
4.

OET Preparation: English for Healthcare Professionals Book 1

Activity 27: Complete the sentences.

waist   groin strain   abdominal   stretch marks

1. Striae are irregular bands of skin, also called _____ seen when a person grows or gains weight rapidly.

2. Adductor or _____ is one of the most common sports injuries, especially football injuries.

3. The _____ to hip ratio is often used in preference to the BMI as a measurement of the risk of obesity and cardiovascular disease.

4. Visceral or _____ fat has been linked to increased risk of Type 2 diabetes.

Medical Terms: Abdominopelvic Region

Term	Latin	Greek
belly / midriff	abdomen	gastro
inner abdomen		koila /celiac
upper abdomen	epigastrium	
navel	umbilicus	omphalos
abdominal wall		laparo
pubic bone	pubic tubercle	

genitals	pubes	

Activity 28: Label the picture.

iliac crest   abdomen   epigastrium   pubes   umbilicus

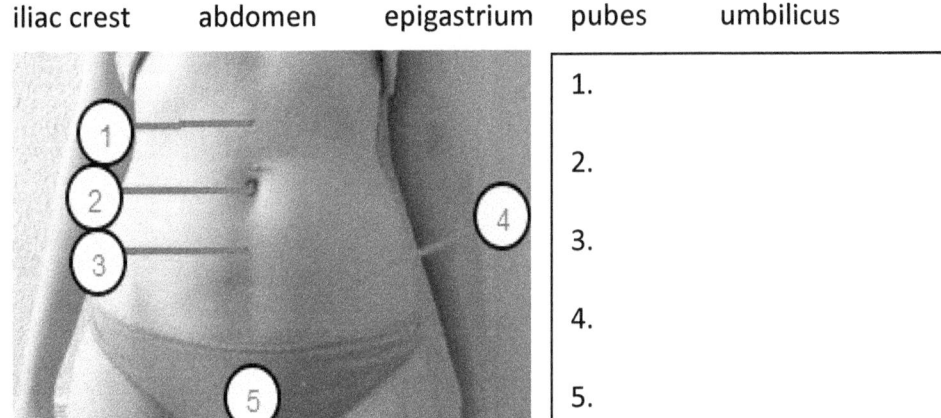

1.
2.
3.
4.
5.

Activity 29: Complete the sentences.

stomach   navel   pubic hair   gastritis

1. Coeliac disease is a syndrome which is characterized by poor absorption of gluten in the _____ and intestines.

2. Epigastric pain may be caused by _____ or inflammation of the stomach lining. This type of pain is also called heartburn.

OET Preparation: English for Healthcare Professionals Book 1

3.An umbilical hernia is a protrusion of the abdominal lining through to the area around the _____.

4. Pediculosis pubis, also called pubic lice, are usually found in the _____ of the genitals and are spread during sexual activity.

Medical Terms: Anterior Knee and Lower Leg

Term	Latin	Greek
leg	crus / cruro	scel / skel
shinbone	tibia	cnem /knem
kneecap	patella	
ankle	talus /astragalus	astragalos
bony prominence on each side of	malleolus	

Virginia Allum

| ankle | | |

Activity 30: Label the picture.

shin   patella   ankle bone
heel   ball of the foot   calf

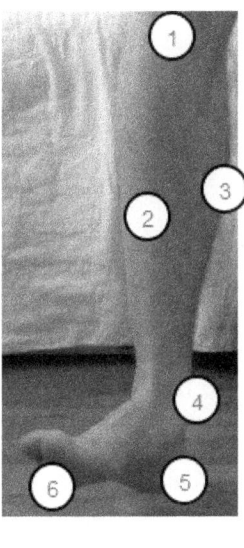

1.

2.

3.

4.

5.

6.

Activity 31: Complete the sentences.

   tibia   knee   kneecap

1. A fractured _____ makes it difficult to weight bear on the affected leg.

2. An ACL tear (Anterior Cruciate Ligament) can cause the _____ to give way, when exercising.

3. An unstable _____ is known as patella subluxation, a condition which can cause extreme pain, when waling or running.

Virginia Allum

Medical Terms: Posterior Lower Leg and Knee

Term	Latin	Greek
calf	sura	
calf bone	fibula	
mid-calf or shank		gastrocnemius muscle
knee	poples / poplites	
knee pit / back of the knee	popliteal fossa	
Achilles tendon	calcaneal tendon	achillo-
heel bone	calcaneus	
heel pad	calcaneal fat pad	
instep	dorsum pedis	
arch of the foot	arcus pedis	
fallen arch or flat foot	pes planus	
high arch	pes cavus	
sole	planta / volar	

OET Preparation: English for Healthcare Professionals Book 1

Activity 32: Label the picture.
back of the thigh   calf   popliteal fossa

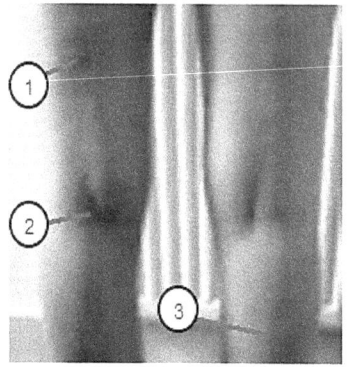

1.

2.

3.

Activity 33: Label the picture.
ball of the foot   ankle   heel pad
arch   sole   ankle bone

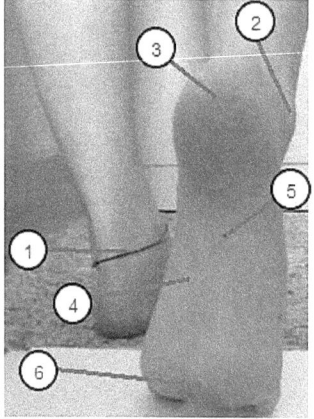

1.

2.

3.

4.

5.

6.

Virginia Allum

The sole of the foot is the complete underside of the foot including the ball of the foot, the arches and the heel pad.

Activity 34: Complete the sentences.

arch   fallen arches   podiatrists   heelbone

1. Allied Health Professionals who treat abnormal conditions of the lower leg are called _____.

2. Pes planus, also known as 'flat feet' or _____ is characterized by the underside of the foot collapsing, so that the whole of the underside of the foot touches the floor when walking, causing foot pain and difficulties with mobilization.

3. The _____ of the foot or *arcus pedis* is important for the foot to be able to support the weight of the body, when standing.

4. Hook-shaped bones that form on the _____ are called heel spurs.

OET Preparation: English for Healthcare Professionals Book 1

Medical Terms: The Foot

Term	Latin	Greek
foot / feet	pes / pedis	pod
instep / top of the foot	dorsum pedis	
toe	digitus pedis	phalanx / phalanges
big toe	hallux	
joint at base of big toe		metatarsal phalangeal joint (MTPJ)
toenail	unguis	onycho

Virginia Allum

Activity 35: Label the picture.

instep   hallux   metatarsal phalangeal joint   toe nail

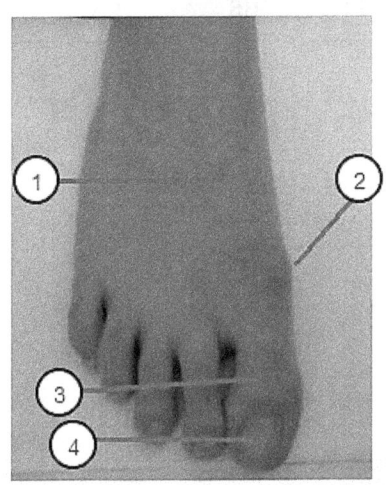

1.
2.
3.
4.

Activity 36: Complete the sentences.

heel pain   calf pain   pronation   ball of the foot

1. The most common cause of _____ is *plantar fasciitis*, inflammation of the band of muscle under the foot.

2. Poor alignment of the foot may cause excessive _____ and reduces the shock absorbency of the foot.

3. Metatarsalgia is the term used to describe pain in the _____ under the metatarsal bones.

4. Injury to the Achilles tendon can cause _____ as well as pain at the back of the heel.

OET Preparation: English for Healthcare Professionals Book 1

Medical Terms: The Arms

Term	Latin	Greek
upper arm	humerus	brachio
forearm	radius and ulna	antebrachium
elbow	cubitus	olene
tip of the elbow		olecranon process
crook of the elbow	cubital fossa	
wrist	carpus	metacarpos
wrist joint	radiocarpal joint	
hand	manus	cheiro / chiro

Note: Anatomical snuffbox: indentation below the thumb near the wrist so-called because this part of the hand was used when sniffing snuff (powdered tobacco)

Activity 37: Label the picture.

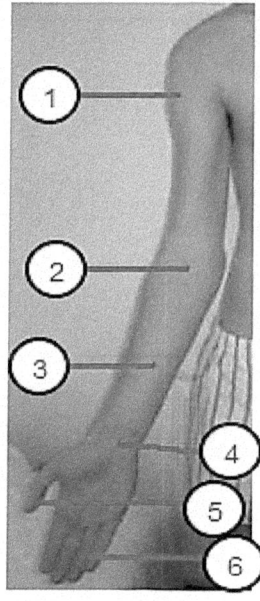

1.
2.
3.
4.
5.
6.

OET Preparation: English for Healthcare Professionals Book 1

Activity 38: Label the picture.

cubital fossa   forearm   olecranon process

1. _____

2. _____

3. _____

Activity 39: Complete the sentences.

radial   median   brachial

1. The _____ pulse is felt at the wrist.

2. Place the stethoscope over the _____ artery in the cubital fossa.

3. Carpal tunnel syndrome is caused by pressure on the _____ nerve in the wrist.

Medical Terms: Back of the Hand

Term	Latin	Greek
back of the hand	dorsum manus	
knuckle	interphalangeal joint	condyle
thumb	pollex / pollicis	
area between thumb and index finger		thenar space
finger	digit	dactyl
fingerbone	phalanx /phalanges	
finger tip	distal phalanx	
index finger	digitus manus secundus	

OET Preparation: English for Healthcare Professionals Book 1

Medical Terms: Palm of the Hand

Term	Latin	Greek
palm	palma / vola manus	
fleshy part near base of thumb		thenar prominence
fleshy part on palm near little finger		hypothenar prominence
finger pad	palmar surface of the finger	
fingertip	distal phalanx	

Virginia Allum

Activity 40: Label the picture.

thenar space   knuckle   finger nail

back of the hand   fingertip   index finger

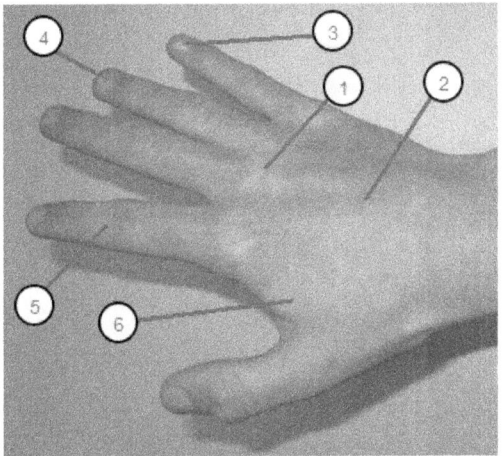

Activity 41: Label The picture.

thenar prominence   distal phalanx   palm

hypothenar prominence   thumb pad

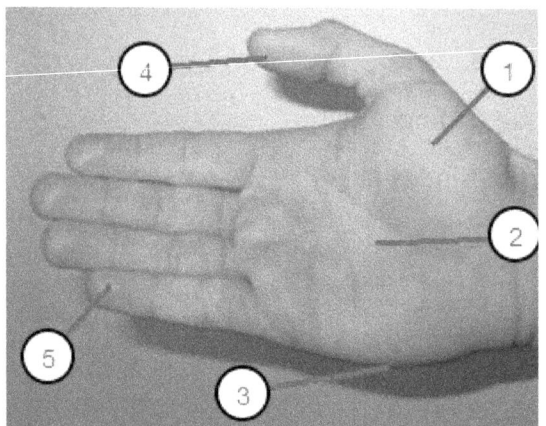

1. _____
2. _____
3. _____
4. _____
5. _____

Activity 42: Diseases and disorders of the hand.
wrist   fingers   fingertips

1. A Colles fracture (broken wrist) is often caused by falling on outstretched hands.

2. Baseball accidents can cause injuries to the extensor digitorum tendon of the _____.

3. Because the _____ are rich with nerves, they are very sensitive.

Medical Terms: Fingernails and Toenails

Term	Latin	Greek
nail	unguis	onycho
nail bed	matrix unguis	onychostroma
half-moon at base of nail	lunula	
cuticle		eponychium
quick		hyponychium
nail border		paronychium

Activity 43: Label the picture.

nail plate   paronychium   lunula   cuticle

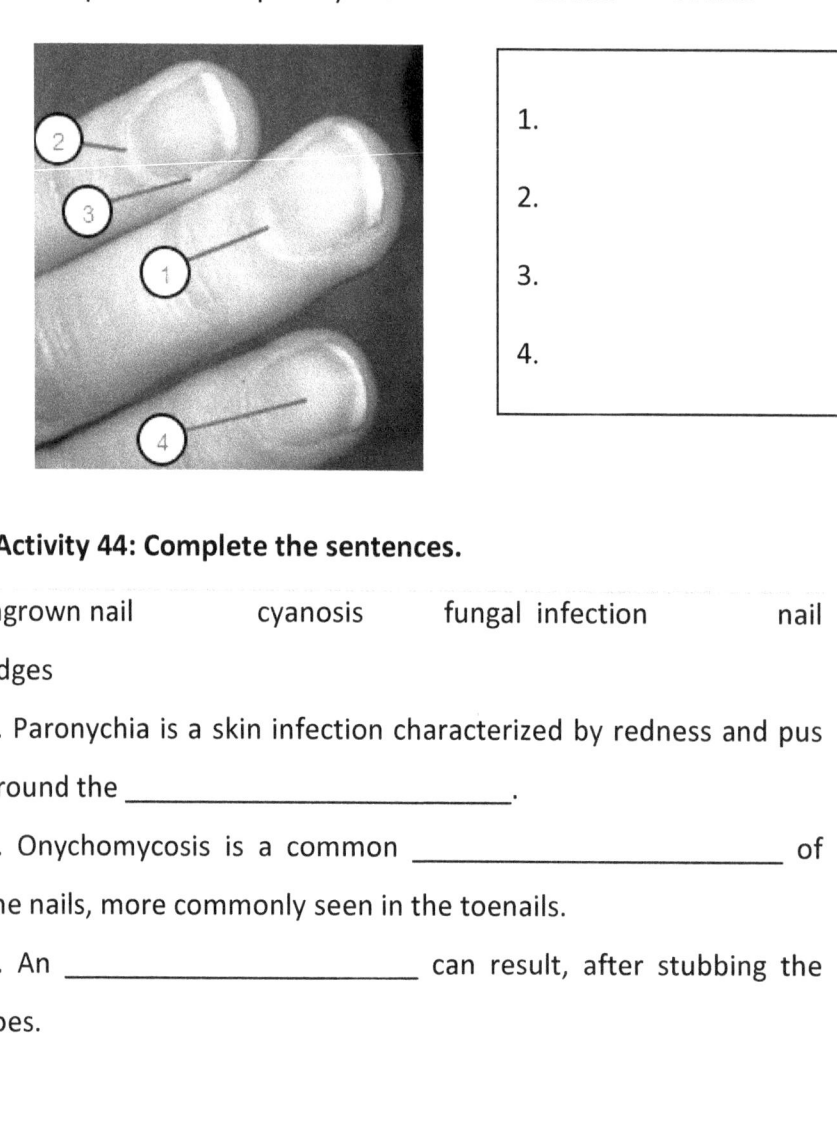

1.
2.
3.
4.

Activity 44: Complete the sentences.

ingrown nail   cyanosis   fungal infection   nail edges

1. Paronychia is a skin infection characterized by redness and pus around the _____.

2. Onychomycosis is a common _____ of the nails, more commonly seen in the toenails.

3. An _____ can result, after stubbing the toes.

4. Blue colouration of the fingernails is one of the signs of _____ , caused by low haemoglobin levels in the blood.

Answers:

Activity 1:

1. mouth ulcers   2. oropharynx   3. stomatitis   4. mouthpiece   5. Mouth breathing

Activity 2:

1.make 2.do 3.take 4.do 5.do 6.take 7.do 8.take 9.do 10.make

Activity 3:

1.a 2.c 3.b 4.e 5.d

Activity 4:

Verbal communication	Non-verbal communication
statements	changing body positions
questions	gestures
commands	eye contact
interjections	tone of voice

OET Preparation: English for Healthcare Professionals Book 1

Medical Terms: The Body

Activity 1:

1. head   2. crown of the head   3. hair   4. forehead

5. temple   6. chin

Activity 2:

1. cephalic   2. trichotillomania   3. craniotomy

4. maxillofacial   5. gnathodynia

Activity 3:

1. crown   2. occiput   3. parietal side   4. ear lobe   5. nape of the neck

Activity 4: 1. crown   2. back   3. nuchal

Activity 5: 1. face   2. cheekbone   3. mouth   4. nose

5. Adam's apple

Activity 6: 1. oral   2. zygoma   3. chin

Activity 7: 1. glabella   2. bridge of the nose   3. ala nasi

4. nasal septum   5. nostril

Activity 8: 1. rhinoplasty   2. nostril   3. nosebleeds

4. epistaxis

Virginia Allum

Activity 9: 1. supratarsal fold   2. sclera   3. pupil   4. iris

Activity 10: 1. eye lid   2. eye brow   3. eye lash   4. canthus

Activity 11: 1. orbit   2. eye   3. eyelid   4. protect

Activity 12: 1. pinna   2. ear lobe   3. cerumen   4. cilia

Activity 13: middle ear. sticky, membrane. tubes, earache. insertion, build-up.

Activity 14: 1. gingiva   2. uvula   3. palate   4. tooth   5. tongue

Activity 15: 1. gums   2. tongue   3. teeth   4. tissue   5. soft palate

Activity 16: 1. clavicle   2. sternum   3. axilla   4. ribs

Activity 17: 1. areola   2. nipple   3. Montgomery tubercles

Activity 18: 1.b   2.a   3.d   4.c

Activity 19: 1. shoulder   2. acromion   3. shoulder blades   4. cervical vertebrae   5. deltoid muscle

Activity 20: 1. subacromial   2. shoulder   3. shoulder blades   4. deltoid

Activity 21: 1. spine   2. lumbar back   3. sacrum   4. dimple of Venus   5. flank

Activity 22: 1. spine   2. childbirth   3. landmarks   4. flank   5. pain

Activity 23: 1. sacrum   2. gluteal cleft   3. gluteal fold   4. cheek

Activity 24: 1. folds   2. gluteal cleft   3. buttocks

Activity 25: 1. waist   2. abdomen   3. buttock   4. striae   5. hip

OET Preparation: English for Healthcare Professionals Book 1

6. external thigh

Activity 26: 1. groin 2. hip   3. outer thigh   4. inner thigh

Activity 27: 1. stretch marks 2.groin strain 3. waist 4.abdominal

Activity 28: 1. epigastrium 2. umbilicus 3. abdomen
4. iliac crest 5. pubes

Activity 29: 1. stomach 2. gastritis   3. navel 4. pubic hair

Activity 30: 1. patella 2. shin 3. calf 4. ankle bone 5. heel
6. ball of the foot

Activity 31: 1. weight bear 2. give way   3.unstable

Activity 32: 1. back of the thigh   2. popliteal fossa 3. calf

Activity 33: 1. ankle   2. ankle bone 3. heel pad   4. arch 5.sole
6.ball of the foot

Activity 34: 1. podiatrists 2. fallen arches 3. arch 4. heel bone

Activity 35: 1. instep 2. metatarsal phalangeal joint 3. hallux
4. toe nail

Activity 36: 1. heel pain 2. pronation 3. ball of the foot 4. calf pain

Activity 37: 1. deltoid muscle 2. cubital fossa 3. forearm   4. wrist
5. thumb 6. finger

Activity 38:   1. olecranon process 2. forearm 3. cubital fossa

Activity 39: 1. radial 2. brachial 3. median

Virginia Allum

Activity 40: 1. knuckle 2. back of the hand 3. finger nail 4. finger tip 5. index finger 6. thenar space

Activity 41: 1. thenar prominence 2. palm 3. hypothenar 4. thumb pad 5. distal phalanx

Activity 42: 1. wrist 2. fingers 3. fingertips

Activity 43: 1. lunula 2. cuticle 3. paronychium 4. nail plate

Activity 44: 1. nail edges 2. fungal infection 3. ingrown nail 4. cyanosis

OET Preparation: English for Healthcare Professionals Book 1

www.ingramcontent.com/pod-product-compliance
Lightning Source LLC
Chambersburg PA
CBHW071407040426
42444CB00009B/2137